50 Baking Basics Recipes for Home

By: Kelly Johnson

Table of Contents

- Classic Chocolate Chip Cookies
- Blueberry Muffins
- Vanilla Cupcakes
- Banana Bread
- Apple Pie
- Lemon Bars
- Cinnamon Rolls
- Pumpkin Bread
- Chocolate Brownies
- Carrot Cake
- Sugar Cookies
- Raspberry Scones
- Oatmeal Raisin Cookies
- Strawberry Shortcake
- Cheesecake
- Peanut Butter Cookies
- Red Velvet Cake
- Lemon Poppy Seed Muffins
- Key Lime Pie
- Snickerdoodles
- Zucchini Bread
- Coconut Macaroons
- Gingerbread Cookies
- Coffee Cake
- Almond Biscotti
- Chocolate Cake
- Pecan Pie
- Shortbread Cookies
- Buttermilk Pancakes
- Marble Cake
- Apple Crisp
- Danish Pastries
- Chocolate Eclairs
- Angel Food Cake
- Fudgy Brownie Bars

- Raspberry Almond Tart
- Pistachio Biscotti
- Blueberry Cobbler
- Black Forest Cake
- Strawberry Swirl Cheesecake
- Chocolate Soufflé
- Lemon Pound Cake
- Maple Pecan Bars
- Cherry Clafoutis
- Almond Joy Cookies
- Irish Soda Bread
- Cranberry Orange Scones
- Chocolate Babka
- Walnut Coffee Cake
- Orange Creamsicle Cupcakes

Classic Chocolate Chip Cookies

Ingredients:

- 1 cup (2 sticks) unsalted butter, softened
- 3/4 cup granulated sugar
- 3/4 cup packed brown sugar
- 2 large eggs
- 1 teaspoon vanilla extract
- 2 1/4 cups all-purpose flour
- 1 teaspoon baking soda
- 1/2 teaspoon salt
- 2 cups semisweet chocolate chips

Instructions:

Preheat your oven to 375°F (190°C). Line baking sheets with parchment paper or silicone baking mats.
In a large mixing bowl, cream together the softened butter, granulated sugar, and brown sugar until light and fluffy.
Beat in the eggs one at a time, then stir in the vanilla extract.
In a separate bowl, whisk together the flour, baking soda, and salt.
Gradually add the dry ingredients to the wet ingredients, mixing until well combined.
Stir in the chocolate chips until evenly distributed throughout the dough.
Using a cookie scoop or spoon, drop rounded tablespoons of dough onto the prepared baking sheets, leaving some space between each cookie.
Bake in the preheated oven for 8 to 10 minutes, or until the edges are lightly golden brown.
Allow the cookies to cool on the baking sheets for a few minutes before transferring them to wire racks to cool completely.
Enjoy your Classic Chocolate Chip Cookies with a glass of milk or your favorite beverage!

Feel free to adjust the amount of chocolate chips or add nuts if desired. These cookies are a classic favorite for a reason – they're soft, chewy, and loaded with delicious chocolatey goodness!

Blueberry Muffins

Ingredients:

- 2 cups all-purpose flour
- 1/2 cup granulated sugar
- 2 teaspoons baking powder
- 1/2 teaspoon baking soda
- 1/4 teaspoon salt
- 1/2 cup unsalted butter, melted and cooled slightly
- 2 large eggs
- 1 cup plain yogurt or sour cream
- 1 teaspoon vanilla extract
- 1 1/2 cups fresh or frozen blueberries
- Optional: 1 tablespoon lemon zest for added flavor

Instructions:

Preheat your oven to 375°F (190°C). Line a muffin tin with paper liners or grease the cups with butter or cooking spray.

In a large mixing bowl, whisk together the flour, sugar, baking powder, baking soda, and salt. If using lemon zest, add it to the dry ingredients and mix well.

In a separate bowl, beat the melted butter, eggs, yogurt or sour cream, and vanilla extract until well combined.

Pour the wet ingredients into the dry ingredients and stir until just combined. Be careful not to overmix; the batter should be lumpy.

Gently fold in the blueberries until evenly distributed throughout the batter.

Using a spoon or cookie scoop, divide the batter evenly among the muffin cups, filling each about two-thirds full.

If desired, sprinkle a little sugar over the tops of the muffins for a crunchy topping.

Bake in the preheated oven for 18 to 22 minutes, or until the muffins are golden brown and a toothpick inserted into the center comes out clean.

Allow the muffins to cool in the pan for a few minutes before transferring them to a wire rack to cool completely.

Enjoy your homemade Blueberry Muffins warm or at room temperature.

These Blueberry Muffins are moist, tender, and bursting with juicy blueberries. They make a delicious breakfast or snack any time of day!

Vanilla Cupcakes

Ingredients:

- 1 1/2 cups all-purpose flour
- 1 1/2 teaspoons baking powder
- 1/4 teaspoon salt
- 1/2 cup (1 stick) unsalted butter, softened
- 3/4 cup granulated sugar
- 2 large eggs, room temperature
- 2 teaspoons vanilla extract
- 1/2 cup milk

Instructions:

Preheat your oven to 350°F (175°C). Line a muffin tin with paper liners.
In a medium bowl, whisk together the flour, baking powder, and salt. Set aside.
In a large mixing bowl, cream together the softened butter and sugar until light and fluffy.
Beat in the eggs, one at a time, mixing well after each addition. Add the vanilla extract and mix until combined.
Gradually add the dry ingredients to the wet ingredients, alternating with the milk, starting and ending with the dry ingredients. Mix until just combined. Be careful not to overmix.
Divide the batter evenly among the muffin cups, filling each about two-thirds full.
Bake in the preheated oven for 18 to 20 minutes, or until a toothpick inserted into the center of a cupcake comes out clean.
Remove the cupcakes from the oven and let them cool in the pan for a few minutes before transferring them to a wire rack to cool completely.
Once the cupcakes are completely cooled, you can frost them with your favorite frosting, decorate as desired, and enjoy!

These Vanilla Cupcakes are perfect for any occasion, from birthday parties to bake sales. They're moist, fluffy, and full of classic vanilla flavor. Feel free to get creative with your frosting and decorations to make them extra special!

Banana Bread

Ingredients:

- 2 to 3 ripe bananas, mashed (about 1 cup)
- 1/3 cup unsalted butter, melted
- 1/2 cup granulated sugar
- 1/4 cup packed brown sugar
- 1 large egg, beaten
- 1 teaspoon vanilla extract
- 1 teaspoon baking soda
- Pinch of salt
- 1 1/2 cups all-purpose flour
- Optional: 1/2 cup chopped nuts (such as walnuts or pecans)
- Optional: 1/2 cup chocolate chips or raisins

Instructions:

Preheat your oven to 350°F (175°C). Grease a 9x5-inch loaf pan or line it with parchment paper.
In a mixing bowl, mash the ripe bananas with a fork until smooth.
Stir in the melted butter until well combined.
Add both granulated sugar and brown sugar to the banana mixture, and mix well.
Add the beaten egg and vanilla extract to the mixture, stirring until fully incorporated.
Sprinkle baking soda and salt over the mixture, and gently stir to combine.
Gradually add the flour to the wet ingredients, stirring until just combined. Do not overmix.
If using nuts, chocolate chips, or raisins, fold them into the batter until evenly distributed.
Pour the batter into the prepared loaf pan, spreading it evenly.
Bake in the preheated oven for 50 to 60 minutes, or until a toothpick inserted into the center comes out clean.
Allow the banana bread to cool in the pan for about 10 minutes before transferring it to a wire rack to cool completely.
Once cooled, slice and serve your delicious homemade banana bread. Enjoy it warm or at room temperature!

This classic Banana Bread recipe yields a moist and flavorful loaf with a lovely golden crust. It's perfect for breakfast, as a snack, or for sharing with friends and family. Feel free to customize it with your favorite add-ins like nuts, chocolate chips, or dried fruit.

Apple Pie

Ingredients:

For the Pie Crust:

- 2 1/2 cups all-purpose flour
- 1 teaspoon salt
- 1 tablespoon granulated sugar
- 1 cup unsalted butter, chilled and cut into small cubes
- 1/4 to 1/2 cup ice water

For the Apple Filling:

- 6 to 7 medium-sized apples (such as Granny Smith or Honeycrisp), peeled, cored, and thinly sliced
- 1/2 cup granulated sugar
- 1/4 cup packed brown sugar
- 1 teaspoon ground cinnamon
- 1/4 teaspoon ground nutmeg
- 2 tablespoons all-purpose flour
- 1 tablespoon lemon juice
- 2 tablespoons unsalted butter, cut into small pieces

For Egg Wash (optional):

- 1 egg, beaten
- 1 tablespoon milk or water

Instructions:

For the Pie Crust:

> In a large mixing bowl, whisk together the flour, salt, and sugar.
> Add the chilled butter cubes to the flour mixture. Using a pastry blender or your fingertips, work the butter into the flour until it resembles coarse crumbs with some larger pea-sized pieces.
> Gradually drizzle in the ice water, 1 tablespoon at a time, and gently mix with a fork until the dough starts to come together. Be careful not to overwork the dough.

Divide the dough into two equal portions and shape each portion into a disk. Wrap each disk tightly in plastic wrap and refrigerate for at least 1 hour, or overnight.

For the Apple Filling:

In a large mixing bowl, combine the sliced apples, granulated sugar, brown sugar, cinnamon, nutmeg, flour, and lemon juice. Toss until the apples are evenly coated.

To Assemble the Pie:

Preheat your oven to 425°F (220°C).
On a lightly floured surface, roll out one disk of chilled pie dough into a circle large enough to fit into a 9-inch pie dish with some overhang.
Carefully transfer the rolled-out dough to the pie dish, gently pressing it into the bottom and sides.
Spoon the prepared apple filling into the pie crust, mounding it slightly in the center. Dot the top of the filling with small pieces of butter.
Roll out the second disk of pie dough and place it over the filling. Trim any excess dough, leaving about a 1-inch overhang. Fold the overhanging dough under itself and crimp the edges to seal.
If desired, create decorative vents in the top crust to allow steam to escape during baking.
Optional: In a small bowl, whisk together the beaten egg and milk or water to make an egg wash. Brush the top crust with the egg wash for a shiny finish.
Place the pie on a baking sheet to catch any drips, and bake in the preheated oven for 45 to 55 minutes, or until the crust is golden brown and the filling is bubbling.
If the crust starts to brown too quickly, you can cover the edges with aluminum foil halfway through baking to prevent burning.
Once baked, remove the pie from the oven and allow it to cool on a wire rack for at least 2 hours before slicing and serving.
Serve slices of homemade Apple Pie warm or at room temperature, optionally topped with vanilla ice cream or whipped cream.

This classic Apple Pie is a timeless dessert perfect for any occasion. With its buttery flaky crust and sweet cinnamon-spiced apple filling, it's sure to be a hit with family and friends!

Lemon Bars

Ingredients:

For the Crust:

- 1 cup all-purpose flour
- 1/2 cup unsalted butter, softened
- 1/4 cup powdered sugar

For the Filling:

- 4 large eggs
- 1 1/2 cups granulated sugar
- 1/4 cup all-purpose flour
- 1/2 cup fresh lemon juice (about 3-4 lemons)
- Zest of 2 lemons
- Powdered sugar, for dusting

Instructions:

Preheat your oven to 350°F (175°C). Grease a 9x13-inch baking dish or line it with parchment paper, leaving some overhang for easy removal.
In a mixing bowl, combine the flour, softened butter, and powdered sugar for the crust. Mix until well combined and crumbly.
Press the crust mixture evenly into the bottom of the prepared baking dish.
Bake the crust in the preheated oven for 15-18 minutes, or until lightly golden brown. Remove from the oven and set aside.
While the crust is baking, prepare the filling. In a separate mixing bowl, whisk together the eggs, granulated sugar, flour, lemon juice, and lemon zest until smooth and well combined.
Pour the filling over the baked crust, spreading it out evenly.
Return the baking dish to the oven and bake for an additional 20-25 minutes, or until the filling is set and the edges are lightly golden brown.
Remove the lemon bars from the oven and allow them to cool completely in the baking dish.
Once cooled, refrigerate the lemon bars for at least 2 hours, or until chilled and firm.

Once chilled, use the parchment paper overhang to lift the lemon bars out of the baking dish. Place them on a cutting board and dust with powdered sugar.
Cut the lemon bars into squares or rectangles using a sharp knife.
Serve and enjoy these deliciously tangy Lemon Bars as a refreshing treat!

These Lemon Bars are perfect for any occasion, from potlucks to picnics. They have a buttery crust and a tangy lemon filling that's sure to delight your taste buds!

Cinnamon Rolls

Ingredients:

- For the dough:
    - 1 cup warm milk (110°F/45°C)
    - 2 1/4 teaspoons active dry yeast
    - 1/2 cup granulated sugar
    - 1/3 cup unsalted butter, melted
    - 2 large eggs
    - 4 1/2 cups all-purpose flour
    - 1 teaspoon salt
- For the filling:
    - 1/3 cup unsalted butter, softened
    - 1 cup packed brown sugar
    - 2 tablespoons ground cinnamon
- For the cream cheese frosting:
    - 1/4 cup unsalted butter, softened
    - 4 ounces cream cheese, softened
    - 1 1/2 cups powdered sugar
    - 1/2 teaspoon vanilla extract
    - Pinch of salt

Instructions:

In a small bowl, dissolve the yeast in warm milk and let it sit for about 5 minutes until frothy.

In a large mixing bowl, combine the yeast mixture with sugar, melted butter, eggs, flour, and salt. Mix until the dough comes together.

Knead the dough on a lightly floured surface for about 5 minutes until smooth and elastic. Place the dough in a greased bowl, cover, and let it rise in a warm place for 1 hour, or until doubled in size.

Punch down the risen dough and roll it out into a rectangle on a floured surface, about 16x21 inches in size.

Spread the softened butter over the dough, leaving a small border around the edges. Sprinkle the brown sugar and cinnamon evenly over the butter.

Starting with the long edge, roll up the dough tightly, and pinch the seam to seal. Cut the roll into 12 equal pieces.

Place the rolls in a greased 9x13-inch baking dish, cover, and let them rise in a warm place for 30 minutes.

Preheat your oven to 350°F (175°C). Bake the cinnamon rolls for 25-30 minutes, or until golden brown.

While the rolls are baking, prepare the cream cheese frosting. In a mixing bowl, beat together the softened butter, cream cheese, powdered sugar, vanilla extract, and salt until smooth and creamy.

Remove the rolls from the oven and let them cool for a few minutes before spreading the frosting over the top.

Serve the warm cinnamon rolls and enjoy!

These recipes will surely satisfy your sweet cravings! Let me know if you need further assistance.

Pumpkin Bread

Ingredients:

- 1 3/4 cups all-purpose flour
- 1 teaspoon baking soda
- 1/2 teaspoon baking powder
- 1 teaspoon ground cinnamon
- 1/2 teaspoon ground nutmeg
- 1/2 teaspoon ground cloves
- 1/2 teaspoon salt
- 1/2 cup unsalted butter, melted
- 1 cup granulated sugar
- 1/4 cup brown sugar, packed
- 2 large eggs
- 1 teaspoon vanilla extract
- 1 cup canned pumpkin puree
- 1/3 cup water

Instructions:

Preheat your oven to 350°F (175°C). Grease and flour a 9x5-inch loaf pan, or line it with parchment paper.

In a medium bowl, whisk together the flour, baking soda, baking powder, cinnamon, nutmeg, cloves, and salt. Set aside.

In a large mixing bowl, beat together the melted butter, granulated sugar, and brown sugar until well combined.

Add the eggs one at a time, beating well after each addition. Stir in the vanilla extract.

Mix in the pumpkin puree until smooth.

Gradually add the dry ingredients to the wet ingredients, alternating with the water, and mixing until just combined. Be careful not to overmix.

Pour the batter into the prepared loaf pan and smooth the top with a spatula.

Bake in the preheated oven for 60 to 70 minutes, or until a toothpick inserted into the center comes out clean.

Allow the pumpkin bread to cool in the pan for 10 minutes before transferring it to a wire rack to cool completely.

Once cooled, slice and serve your delicious homemade Pumpkin Bread. Enjoy it plain or with a dollop of whipped cream or cream cheese spread!

This Pumpkin Bread is moist, flavorful, and perfect for enjoying during the fall season or any time of the year. Feel free to add chopped nuts or chocolate chips for extra texture and flavor if desired.

Chocolate Brownies

Ingredients:

- 1 cup (2 sticks) unsalted butter
- 2 cups granulated sugar
- 4 large eggs
- 1 teaspoon vanilla extract
- 1 cup all-purpose flour
- 3/4 cup unsweetened cocoa powder
- 1/2 teaspoon salt
- 1 cup chocolate chips or chopped chocolate (optional)

Instructions:

Preheat your oven to 350°F (175°C). Grease a 9x13-inch baking pan or line it with parchment paper.

In a medium saucepan, melt the butter over low heat. Remove from heat and let it cool slightly.

Stir in the granulated sugar until well combined.

Add the eggs one at a time, mixing well after each addition. Stir in the vanilla extract.

In a separate bowl, sift together the flour, cocoa powder, and salt.

Gradually add the dry ingredients to the wet ingredients, mixing until just combined. Be careful not to overmix.

If using, fold in the chocolate chips or chopped chocolate until evenly distributed in the batter.

Pour the batter into the prepared baking pan and spread it out evenly with a spatula.

Bake in the preheated oven for 25-30 minutes, or until a toothpick inserted into the center comes out with a few moist crumbs.

Allow the brownies to cool completely in the pan on a wire rack before cutting into squares.

Serve and enjoy your homemade Chocolate Brownies! They're perfect on their own or served with a scoop of ice cream.

These Chocolate Brownies are rich, fudgy, and irresistible. Feel free to customize them by adding nuts, caramel swirls, or your favorite toppings. Enjoy!

Carrot Cake

Ingredients:

For the cake:

- 2 cups all-purpose flour
- 2 cups grated carrots
- 1 cup granulated sugar
- 1 cup vegetable oil
- 3 large eggs
- 1 teaspoon baking powder
- 1 teaspoon baking soda
- 1 teaspoon ground cinnamon
- 1/2 teaspoon ground nutmeg
- 1/2 teaspoon salt

For the cream cheese frosting:

- 8 oz cream cheese, softened
- 1/2 cup unsalted butter, softened
- 2 cups powdered sugar
- 1 teaspoon vanilla extract

Instructions:

Preheat your oven to 350°F (175°C). Grease and flour a 9x13 inch baking pan, or line it with parchment paper.
In a large mixing bowl, combine the grated carrots, sugar, and vegetable oil. Mix well.
Add the eggs one at a time, mixing well after each addition.
In a separate bowl, sift together the flour, baking powder, baking soda, cinnamon, nutmeg, and salt.
Gradually add the dry ingredients to the wet ingredients, mixing until just combined. Be careful not to overmix.
Pour the batter into the prepared baking pan and spread it out evenly.

Bake in the preheated oven for 35-40 minutes, or until a toothpick inserted into the center of the cake comes out clean.

Allow the cake to cool completely in the pan on a wire rack before frosting.

To make the cream cheese frosting, beat together the softened cream cheese and butter until smooth and creamy.

Gradually add the powdered sugar, mixing well after each addition, until the frosting is smooth and fluffy.

Mix in the vanilla extract.

Once the cake has cooled, spread the cream cheese frosting evenly over the top.

Cut into squares and serve. Enjoy your delicious homemade carrot cake!

Sugar Cookies

Ingredients:

- 2 3/4 cups all-purpose flour
- 1 teaspoon baking soda
- 1/2 teaspoon baking powder
- 1 cup unsalted butter, softened
- 1 1/2 cups white sugar
- 1 egg
- 1 teaspoon vanilla extract

Instructions:

> Preheat your oven to 375°F (190°C).
> In a small bowl, mix together flour, baking soda, and baking powder. Set aside.
> In a large bowl, cream together the butter and sugar until smooth. Beat in the egg and vanilla.
> Gradually blend in the dry ingredients.
> Roll rounded teaspoonfuls of dough into balls, and place onto ungreased cookie sheets.
> Bake 8 to 10 minutes in the preheated oven, or until golden. Let cookies cool on the baking sheet for a few minutes before transferring to wire racks to cool completely.
> Once cooled, you can decorate the cookies with icing, sprinkles, or any other desired toppings.

Feel free to get creative with shapes and decorations. Enjoy your homemade sugar cookies!

Raspberry Scones

Ingredients:

- 2 cups all-purpose flour
- 1/3 cup granulated sugar
- 1 tablespoon baking powder
- 1/2 teaspoon salt
- 1/2 cup unsalted butter, cold and cut into small pieces
- 1 cup fresh raspberries
- 1/2 cup heavy cream, plus more for brushing
- 1 large egg
- 1 teaspoon vanilla extract

Instructions:

Preheat your oven to 400°F (200°C). Line a baking sheet with parchment paper or lightly grease it.
In a large mixing bowl, whisk together the flour, sugar, baking powder, and salt.
Cut in the cold butter using a pastry cutter or your fingers until the mixture resembles coarse crumbs.
Gently fold in the raspberries, being careful not to crush them.
In a separate small bowl, whisk together the heavy cream, egg, and vanilla extract.
Add the cream mixture to the dry ingredients and stir until just combined. Be careful not to overmix.
Turn the dough out onto a lightly floured surface and gently knead it a few times until it comes together.
Pat the dough into a circle about 1 inch (2.5 cm) thick. Cut the circle into 8 wedges.
Place the scones on the prepared baking sheet, leaving some space between each one.
Lightly brush the tops of the scones with heavy cream.
Bake for 15-18 minutes, or until the scones are golden brown and cooked through.
Allow the scones to cool on the baking sheet for a few minutes before transferring them to a wire rack to cool completely.
Serve the raspberry scones warm or at room temperature, optionally with clotted cream or jam.

Enjoy your homemade raspberry scones!

Oatmeal Raisin Cookies

Ingredients:

- 1 cup unsalted butter, softened
- 1 cup packed brown sugar
- 1/2 cup granulated sugar
- 2 large eggs
- 1 teaspoon vanilla extract
- 1 1/2 cups all-purpose flour
- 1 teaspoon baking soda
- 1 teaspoon ground cinnamon
- 1/2 teaspoon salt
- 3 cups old-fashioned rolled oats
- 1 cup raisins

Instructions:

Preheat your oven to 350°F (175°C). Line baking sheets with parchment paper or lightly grease them.
In a large mixing bowl, cream together the softened butter, brown sugar, and granulated sugar until light and fluffy.
Beat in the eggs, one at a time, then stir in the vanilla extract.
In a separate bowl, whisk together the flour, baking soda, cinnamon, and salt.
Gradually add the dry ingredients to the creamed mixture and mix until well combined.
Stir in the rolled oats and raisins until evenly distributed throughout the dough.
Drop dough by rounded tablespoons onto the prepared baking sheets, spacing them about 2 inches apart.
Flatten the dough slightly with the back of a spoon or your fingers.
Bake in the preheated oven for 10 to 12 minutes, or until the edges are golden brown.
Allow the cookies to cool on the baking sheets for a few minutes before transferring them to wire racks to cool completely.
Store the oatmeal raisin cookies in an airtight container at room temperature for up to a week.

Enjoy these delicious oatmeal raisin cookies with a glass of milk or a cup of tea!

Strawberry Shortcake

Ingredients:

For the biscuits:

- 2 cups all-purpose flour
- 1/4 cup granulated sugar
- 1 tablespoon baking powder
- 1/2 teaspoon salt
- 1/2 cup unsalted butter, cold and cut into small pieces
- 3/4 cup milk
- 1 teaspoon vanilla extract

For the strawberries:

- 4 cups fresh strawberries, hulled and sliced
- 1/4 cup granulated sugar (adjust according to the sweetness of strawberries)
- 1 tablespoon lemon juice

For the whipped cream:

- 1 cup heavy whipping cream
- 2 tablespoons powdered sugar
- 1 teaspoon vanilla extract

Instructions:

For the biscuits:

> Preheat your oven to 425°F (220°C). Line a baking sheet with parchment paper.
> In a large mixing bowl, combine the flour, sugar, baking powder, and salt.
> Cut in the cold butter using a pastry cutter or your fingers until the mixture resembles coarse crumbs.
> Stir in the milk and vanilla extract until just combined.
> Turn the dough out onto a lightly floured surface and pat it into a rectangle about 1/2 inch (1.25 cm) thick.
> Use a biscuit cutter or a glass to cut out rounds of dough. Place them on the prepared baking sheet.
> Bake for 12-15 minutes, or until the biscuits are golden brown.
> Allow the biscuits to cool on a wire rack.

For the strawberries:

> In a medium bowl, combine the sliced strawberries, granulated sugar, and lemon juice. Stir gently to coat the strawberries in sugar.
> Let the strawberries sit at room temperature for about 30 minutes, stirring occasionally, until they release their juices.

For the whipped cream:

> In a large mixing bowl, whip the heavy cream, powdered sugar, and vanilla extract until stiff peaks form.

Assembling the strawberry shortcake:

> Slice the cooled biscuits in half horizontally.
> Place a spoonful of strawberries on the bottom half of each biscuit.
> Top the strawberries with a dollop of whipped cream.
> Place the other half of the biscuit on top.
> Garnish with additional strawberries and whipped cream if desired.
> Serve immediately and enjoy!

Strawberry shortcake is best enjoyed fresh, but you can store leftover components separately in the refrigerator and assemble just before serving.

Cheesecake

Ingredients:

For the crust:

- 1 1/2 cups graham cracker crumbs
- 1/4 cup granulated sugar
- 1/2 cup unsalted butter, melted

For the filling:

- 4 (8-ounce) packages cream cheese, softened
- 1 1/4 cups granulated sugar
- 4 large eggs
- 1 cup sour cream
- 1 teaspoon vanilla extract
- 2 tablespoons all-purpose flour

For the topping (optional):

- Fresh fruit, fruit preserves, or whipped cream for garnish

Instructions:

For the crust:

Preheat your oven to 325°F (160°C). Grease a 9-inch springform pan.
In a medium bowl, mix together the graham cracker crumbs, sugar, and melted butter until well combined.
Press the mixture firmly onto the bottom of the prepared springform pan.
Bake the crust in the preheated oven for 10 minutes. Remove from the oven and set aside to cool.

For the filling:

In a large mixing bowl, beat the cream cheese and sugar together until smooth and creamy.
Add the eggs, one at a time, beating well after each addition.
Mix in the sour cream and vanilla extract until well combined.
Add the flour and mix until just incorporated.
Pour the filling over the cooled crust in the springform pan.

Baking:

Wrap the bottom of the springform pan with aluminum foil to prevent any water from seeping in.

Place the springform pan in a larger baking pan and fill the larger pan with hot water to create a water bath (about halfway up the sides of the springform pan).

Bake the cheesecake in the preheated oven for 55-60 minutes, or until the edges are set and the center is slightly jiggly.

Turn off the oven and let the cheesecake cool in the oven with the door closed for 1 hour.

Remove the cheesecake from the oven and allow it to cool completely at room temperature.

Once cooled, refrigerate the cheesecake for at least 4 hours, preferably overnight, to set.

Serving:

Before serving, run a knife around the edges of the springform pan to loosen the cheesecake.

Remove the outer ring of the springform pan.

If desired, top the cheesecake with fresh fruit, fruit preserves, or whipped cream before slicing and serving.

Enjoy this creamy and delicious New York-style cheesecake with your favorite toppings!

Peanut Butter Cookies

Ingredients:

- 1/2 cup unsalted butter, softened
- 1/2 cup granulated sugar
- 1/2 cup packed brown sugar
- 1/2 cup creamy peanut butter
- 1 large egg
- 1 teaspoon vanilla extract
- 1 1/4 cups all-purpose flour
- 1/2 teaspoon baking powder
- 1/2 teaspoon baking soda
- 1/4 teaspoon salt

Instructions:

Preheat your oven to 350°F (175°C). Line baking sheets with parchment paper or lightly grease them.
In a large mixing bowl, cream together the softened butter, granulated sugar, brown sugar, and peanut butter until light and fluffy.
Beat in the egg and vanilla extract until well combined.
In a separate bowl, whisk together the flour, baking powder, baking soda, and salt.
Gradually add the dry ingredients to the wet ingredients, mixing until just combined. Do not overmix.
Roll the dough into 1-inch balls and place them on the prepared baking sheets, spacing them about 2 inches apart.
Use a fork to flatten each ball of dough, creating a crisscross pattern on top.
Bake in the preheated oven for 10-12 minutes, or until the cookies are lightly golden around the edges.
Allow the cookies to cool on the baking sheets for a few minutes before transferring them to wire racks to cool completely.
Once cooled, store the peanut butter cookies in an airtight container at room temperature.

Enjoy these delicious and chewy peanut butter cookies with a glass of milk or your favorite beverage!

Red Velvet Cake

Ingredients:

For the cake:

- 2 1/2 cups all-purpose flour
- 1 1/2 cups granulated sugar
- 1 teaspoon baking soda
- 1 teaspoon salt
- 1 teaspoon cocoa powder
- 1 1/2 cups vegetable oil
- 1 cup buttermilk, room temperature
- 2 large eggs, room temperature
- 2 tablespoons red food coloring
- 1 teaspoon vanilla extract
- 1 teaspoon distilled white vinegar

For the cream cheese frosting:

- 16 ounces cream cheese, softened
- 1/2 cup unsalted butter, softened
- 4 cups powdered sugar, sifted
- 1 teaspoon vanilla extract

Instructions:

For the cake:

Preheat your oven to 350°F (175°C). Grease and flour two 9-inch round cake pans.
In a medium bowl, sift together the flour, sugar, baking soda, salt, and cocoa powder.
In a large mixing bowl, whisk together the vegetable oil, buttermilk, eggs, red food coloring, vanilla extract, and vinegar until well combined.
Gradually add the dry ingredients to the wet ingredients, mixing until smooth and well combined.
Divide the batter evenly between the prepared cake pans.
Bake in the preheated oven for 25-30 minutes, or until a toothpick inserted into the center of the cakes comes out clean.

Remove the cakes from the oven and let them cool in the pans for 10 minutes before transferring them to wire racks to cool completely.

For the cream cheese frosting:

In a large mixing bowl, beat the cream cheese and butter together until smooth and creamy.
Gradually add the powdered sugar, one cup at a time, beating well after each addition.
Stir in the vanilla extract until well combined.

Assembling the cake:

Once the cakes are completely cooled, place one cake layer on a serving plate.
Spread a layer of cream cheese frosting over the top of the cake layer.
Place the second cake layer on top and spread a thin layer of frosting over the entire cake to create a crumb coat.
Chill the cake in the refrigerator for 30 minutes to set the crumb coat.
Once set, frost the entire cake with the remaining cream cheese frosting.
Decorate the cake as desired.

Enjoy this classic red velvet cake with its signature cream cheese frosting!

Lemon Poppy Seed Muffins

Ingredients:

- 2 cups all-purpose flour
- 1/2 cup granulated sugar
- 1/4 cup packed brown sugar
- 2 tablespoons poppy seeds
- 1 tablespoon baking powder
- 1/2 teaspoon baking soda
- 1/4 teaspoon salt
- 3/4 cup unsalted butter, melted and cooled
- 3/4 cup sour cream
- 2 large eggs
- 1/4 cup fresh lemon juice
- Zest of 2 lemons
- 1 teaspoon vanilla extract

For the Glaze (optional):

- 1 cup powdered sugar
- 2-3 tablespoons fresh lemon juice

Instructions:

Preheat your oven to 375°F (190°C). Line a muffin tin with paper liners or grease them lightly.
In a large mixing bowl, whisk together the flour, granulated sugar, brown sugar, poppy seeds, baking powder, baking soda, and salt.
In another bowl, whisk together the melted butter, sour cream, eggs, lemon juice, lemon zest, and vanilla extract until well combined.
Pour the wet ingredients into the dry ingredients and gently fold together until just combined. Be careful not to overmix; a few lumps are okay.
Spoon the batter into the prepared muffin cups, filling each about 2/3 full.
Bake in the preheated oven for 18-20 minutes, or until a toothpick inserted into the center of a muffin comes out clean.
Allow the muffins to cool in the tin for a few minutes, then transfer them to a wire rack to cool completely.

For the Glaze (optional):

In a small bowl, whisk together the powdered sugar and lemon juice until smooth.
Drizzle the glaze over the cooled muffins.

Enjoy these delicious lemon poppy seed muffins with a cup of tea or coffee!

Key Lime Pie

Ingredients:

For the crust:

- 1 1/2 cups graham cracker crumbs
- 1/4 cup granulated sugar
- 6 tablespoons unsalted butter, melted

For the filling:

- 3 large egg yolks
- 1 (14-ounce) can sweetened condensed milk
- 1/2 cup fresh Key lime juice (regular lime juice can be used as a substitute)
- Zest of 1 lime (optional)

For the topping (optional):

- Whipped cream
- Lime slices or zest for garnish

Instructions:

For the crust:

> Preheat your oven to 350°F (175°C).
> In a medium bowl, combine the graham cracker crumbs, granulated sugar, and melted butter until well mixed.
> Press the mixture firmly into the bottom and up the sides of a 9-inch pie dish.
> Bake the crust in the preheated oven for 10 minutes. Remove from the oven and let it cool while you prepare the filling.

For the filling:

> In a large mixing bowl, beat the egg yolks until they become thick and pale in color.
> Gradually add the sweetened condensed milk, continuing to beat until well combined.
> Slowly pour in the Key lime juice, stirring until the mixture is smooth and well incorporated. Be careful not to overmix.
> If desired, stir in the lime zest for an extra burst of flavor.

Assembling and baking the pie:

> Pour the filling into the cooled graham cracker crust, spreading it evenly with a spatula.

Bake the pie in the preheated oven for 15-20 minutes, or until the filling is set and just beginning to brown around the edges.

Remove the pie from the oven and let it cool to room temperature.

Once cooled, refrigerate the pie for at least 2 hours, or until thoroughly chilled and set.

Serving:

Before serving, garnish the pie with whipped cream and lime slices or zest, if desired.

Slice and serve the Key lime pie chilled.

Enjoy this tangy and creamy Key lime pie as a refreshing dessert!

Snickerdoodles

Ingredients:

For the cookie dough:

- 1 cup unsalted butter, softened
- 1 1/2 cups granulated sugar
- 2 large eggs
- 2 3/4 cups all-purpose flour
- 2 teaspoons cream of tartar
- 1 teaspoon baking soda
- 1/4 teaspoon salt

For rolling:

- 1/4 cup granulated sugar
- 2 tablespoons ground cinnamon

Instructions:

Preheat your oven to 375°F (190°C). Line baking sheets with parchment paper or lightly grease them.
In a large mixing bowl, cream together the softened butter and 1 1/2 cups granulated sugar until light and fluffy.
Add the eggs, one at a time, beating well after each addition.
In a separate bowl, sift together the flour, cream of tartar, baking soda, and salt.
Gradually add the dry ingredients to the creamed mixture, mixing until just combined. Do not overmix.
In a small bowl, mix together the 1/4 cup granulated sugar and ground cinnamon for rolling the cookies.
Shape the dough into 1-inch balls and roll each ball in the cinnamon-sugar mixture until coated.
Place the coated dough balls onto the prepared baking sheets, spacing them about 2 inches apart.
Using the bottom of a glass, flatten each dough ball slightly.
Bake the cookies in the preheated oven for 8 to 10 minutes, or until the edges are lightly golden but the centers are still soft.
Allow the cookies to cool on the baking sheets for a few minutes before transferring them to wire racks to cool completely.
Store the snickerdoodles in an airtight container at room temperature.

Enjoy these classic snickerdoodle cookies with a glass of milk or your favorite hot beverage!

Zucchini Bread

Ingredients:

- 2 cups grated zucchini (about 2 medium zucchinis)
- 2 cups all-purpose flour
- 1 teaspoon baking powder
- 1/2 teaspoon baking soda
- 1/2 teaspoon salt
- 1 teaspoon ground cinnamon
- 1/2 teaspoon ground nutmeg
- 2 large eggs
- 1 cup granulated sugar
- 1/2 cup vegetable oil or melted butter
- 1 teaspoon vanilla extract
- Optional: 1/2 cup chopped nuts (such as walnuts or pecans), 1/2 cup raisins or chocolate chips

Instructions:

Preheat your oven to 350°F (175°C). Grease and flour a 9x5-inch loaf pan or line it with parchment paper.

Place the grated zucchini in a clean kitchen towel and squeeze out excess moisture. Set aside.

In a large mixing bowl, whisk together the flour, baking powder, baking soda, salt, cinnamon, and nutmeg.

In another bowl, beat the eggs until light and frothy. Add the sugar, oil or melted butter, and vanilla extract, and mix until well combined.

Stir the grated zucchini into the wet ingredients.

Gradually add the dry ingredients to the wet ingredients, mixing until just combined. Be careful not to overmix.

If using, fold in the chopped nuts, raisins, or chocolate chips.

Pour the batter into the prepared loaf pan and spread it out evenly.

Bake in the preheated oven for 50 to 60 minutes, or until a toothpick inserted into the center of the bread comes out clean.

Remove the zucchini bread from the oven and let it cool in the pan for 10 minutes.

After 10 minutes, remove the bread from the pan and transfer it to a wire rack to cool completely.

Once cooled, slice and serve the zucchini bread. Enjoy it plain or with a smear of butter or cream cheese.

Store any leftover zucchini bread in an airtight container at room temperature for up to 3 days, or freeze it for longer storage.

Coconut Macaroons

Ingredients:

- 3 cups sweetened shredded coconut
- 2/3 cup granulated sugar
- 1/4 teaspoon salt
- 4 large egg whites
- 1 teaspoon vanilla extract
- Optional: 1/2 cup chocolate chips or melted chocolate for dipping (if desired)

Instructions:

Preheat your oven to 325°F (160°C). Line a baking sheet with parchment paper or a silicone baking mat.
In a large mixing bowl, combine the sweetened shredded coconut, granulated sugar, and salt.
In a separate bowl, whisk the egg whites and vanilla extract until slightly frothy.
Pour the egg whites mixture over the coconut mixture and stir until well combined.
Using a spoon or a cookie scoop, scoop out portions of the coconut mixture and drop them onto the prepared baking sheet, spacing them about 2 inches apart. Use your fingers or the back of a spoon to shape the mounds into compact rounds.
Bake in the preheated oven for 20-25 minutes, or until the macaroons are golden brown around the edges.
Remove the baking sheet from the oven and let the macaroons cool on the pan for a few minutes before transferring them to a wire rack to cool completely.
If desired, melt the chocolate chips in a microwave or over a double boiler, then dip the bottoms of the cooled macaroons into the melted chocolate or drizzle chocolate over the tops.
Place the dipped or drizzled macaroons back onto the parchment paper or baking mat to allow the chocolate to set.
Once the chocolate has set, serve and enjoy your coconut macaroons!

These coconut macaroons are perfect for enjoying as a sweet treat or for sharing with friends and family. Store any leftovers in an airtight container at room temperature for up to a week.

Gingerbread Cookies

Ingredients:

For the cookie dough:

- 3 cups all-purpose flour
- 1 teaspoon baking soda
- 1/4 teaspoon salt
- 1 tablespoon ground ginger
- 1 1/2 teaspoons ground cinnamon
- 1/4 teaspoon ground cloves
- 1/2 cup unsalted butter, softened
- 1/2 cup packed brown sugar
- 1 large egg
- 1/2 cup molasses
- 1 teaspoon vanilla extract

For decorating (optional):

- Royal icing
- Assorted sprinkles or candy decorations

Instructions:

In a medium bowl, whisk together the flour, baking soda, salt, ginger, cinnamon, and cloves. Set aside.

In a large mixing bowl, cream together the softened butter and brown sugar until light and fluffy.

Add the egg, molasses, and vanilla extract to the creamed butter mixture, and beat until well combined.

Gradually add the dry ingredients to the wet ingredients, mixing until a dough forms. If the dough is too sticky, you can add a little more flour, one tablespoon at a time, until it reaches the right consistency.

Divide the dough into two equal portions, flatten each portion into a disc, and wrap them in plastic wrap. Chill the dough in the refrigerator for at least 1 hour, or until firm.

Preheat your oven to 350°F (175°C). Line baking sheets with parchment paper or silicone baking mats.

On a lightly floured surface, roll out one disc of chilled dough to about 1/4 inch thickness. Use gingerbread cookie cutters to cut out shapes from the dough.

Place the cut-out cookies onto the prepared baking sheets, spacing them about 1 inch apart.

Gather any scraps of dough, reroll them, and cut out more cookies until all the dough is used.

Bake the cookies in the preheated oven for 8-10 minutes, or until the edges are firm. The cookies will firm up more as they cool.

Remove the cookies from the oven and let them cool on the baking sheets for a few minutes before transferring them to wire racks to cool completely.

Decorating (optional):

- Once the cookies are completely cooled, you can decorate them with royal icing and assorted sprinkles or candy decorations.
- Allow the icing to set before serving or storing the cookies.

Enjoy these delicious gingerbread cookies as a festive treat or as decorations for your holiday celebrations!

Coffee Cake

Ingredients:

For the cake:

- 2 cups all-purpose flour
- 1 cup granulated sugar
- 1 teaspoon baking powder
- 1/2 teaspoon baking soda
- 1/2 teaspoon salt
- 1/2 cup unsalted butter, softened
- 1 cup sour cream
- 2 large eggs
- 1 teaspoon vanilla extract

For the streusel topping:

- 1/2 cup packed brown sugar
- 1/2 cup all-purpose flour
- 1 teaspoon ground cinnamon
- 1/4 cup unsalted butter, melted

For the optional glaze:

- 1/2 cup powdered sugar
- 1-2 tablespoons milk
- 1/2 teaspoon vanilla extract

Instructions:

For the streusel topping:

In a small bowl, combine the brown sugar, flour, and cinnamon.
Stir in the melted butter until the mixture resembles coarse crumbs. Set aside.

For the cake:

Preheat your oven to 350°F (175°C). Grease and flour a 9x13-inch baking dish.
In a medium bowl, whisk together the flour, sugar, baking powder, baking soda, and salt.

In a large mixing bowl, cream together the softened butter and sour cream until smooth.

Beat in the eggs, one at a time, then stir in the vanilla extract.

Gradually add the dry ingredients to the wet ingredients, mixing until well combined.

Spread the batter evenly into the prepared baking dish.

Assembly:

Sprinkle the streusel topping evenly over the cake batter.

Bake in the preheated oven for 25-30 minutes, or until a toothpick inserted into the center comes out clean.

Allow the coffee cake to cool in the baking dish for at least 10 minutes before serving.

Optional glaze:

In a small bowl, whisk together the powdered sugar, milk, and vanilla extract until smooth.

Drizzle the glaze over the warm coffee cake.

Serve the coffee cake warm or at room temperature.

Enjoy this delicious coffee cake with your favorite hot beverage for a cozy treat!

Almond Biscotti

Ingredients:

- 2 cups all-purpose flour
- 1 cup granulated sugar
- 1 teaspoon baking powder
- 1/4 teaspoon salt
- 3 large eggs
- 1 teaspoon vanilla extract
- 1 teaspoon almond extract
- 1 cup whole almonds, toasted and roughly chopped

Instructions:

Preheat your oven to 350°F (175°C). Line a baking sheet with parchment paper.
In a large mixing bowl, whisk together the flour, sugar, baking powder, and salt.
In a separate bowl, beat the eggs with the vanilla extract and almond extract until well combined.
Gradually add the egg mixture to the dry ingredients, stirring until a dough forms.
Fold in the chopped almonds until evenly distributed throughout the dough.
Divide the dough in half. On a lightly floured surface, shape each half into a log about 12 inches long and 2 inches wide.
Place the logs on the prepared baking sheet, spacing them a few inches apart.
Bake in the preheated oven for 25-30 minutes, or until the logs are firm to the touch and lightly golden brown.
Remove the baking sheet from the oven and let the logs cool for about 10 minutes.
Using a sharp knife, slice the logs diagonally into 1/2-inch thick slices.
Arrange the biscotti cut side down on the baking sheet and return them to the oven.
Bake for an additional 10-15 minutes, or until the biscotti are golden brown and crisp.
Remove the biscotti from the oven and let them cool completely on a wire rack.

Enjoy these delicious almond biscotti with a cup of coffee or tea, or package them up as homemade gifts for friends and family!

Chocolate Cake

Ingredients:

For the cake:

- 1 and 3/4 cups all-purpose flour
- 3/4 cup unsweetened cocoa powder
- 2 cups granulated sugar
- 1 and 1/2 teaspoons baking powder
- 1 and 1/2 teaspoons baking soda
- 1 teaspoon salt
- 2 large eggs
- 1 cup whole milk
- 1/2 cup vegetable oil
- 2 teaspoons vanilla extract
- 1 cup boiling water

For the chocolate frosting:

- 1 cup unsalted butter, softened
- 3 and 1/2 cups powdered sugar
- 1/2 cup unsweetened cocoa powder
- 1/2 teaspoon salt
- 2 teaspoons vanilla extract
- 4-6 tablespoons whole milk or heavy cream

Instructions:

For the cake:

Preheat your oven to 350°F (175°C). Grease and flour two 9-inch round cake pans or line them with parchment paper.
In a large mixing bowl, sift together the flour, cocoa powder, granulated sugar, baking powder, baking soda, and salt.
Add the eggs, milk, oil, and vanilla extract to the dry ingredients. Beat on medium speed until well combined, about 2 minutes.
Stir in the boiling water until the batter is smooth. The batter will be thin, but this is normal.
Divide the batter evenly between the prepared cake pans.

Bake in the preheated oven for 30 to 35 minutes, or until a toothpick inserted into the center of the cakes comes out clean.

Remove the cakes from the oven and let them cool in the pans for 10 minutes. Then, transfer them to wire racks to cool completely before frosting.

For the chocolate frosting:

In a large mixing bowl, beat the softened butter until creamy.

Gradually add the powdered sugar, cocoa powder, salt, vanilla extract, and milk or cream, beating until smooth and creamy. Add more milk or cream as needed to reach your desired consistency.

Once the cakes have cooled completely, place one cake layer on a serving plate or cake stand. Spread a layer of frosting over the top of the cake layer.

Place the second cake layer on top and spread the remaining frosting over the top and sides of the cake.

Optionally, decorate the cake with chocolate shavings, sprinkles, or fresh berries. Slice and serve the chocolate cake, and enjoy!

This chocolate cake is moist, decadent, and perfect for any occasion.

Pecan Pie

Ingredients:

For the pie crust:

- 1 1/4 cups all-purpose flour
- 1/2 teaspoon salt
- 1/2 cup unsalted butter, chilled and cubed
- 1/4 cup ice water

For the filling:

- 1 cup granulated sugar
- 1 cup light corn syrup
- 3 large eggs
- 2 tablespoons unsalted butter, melted
- 1 teaspoon vanilla extract
- 1/4 teaspoon salt
- 1 1/2 cups pecan halves

Instructions:

For the pie crust:

In a large mixing bowl, whisk together the flour and salt.
Add the chilled, cubed butter to the flour mixture.
Use a pastry cutter or your fingers to cut the butter into the flour until the mixture resembles coarse crumbs.
Gradually add the ice water, 1 tablespoon at a time, mixing until the dough comes together.
Shape the dough into a disk, wrap it in plastic wrap, and refrigerate for at least 1 hour.

For the filling:

Preheat your oven to 375°F (190°C).
Roll out the chilled pie crust on a lightly floured surface to fit a 9-inch pie dish. Trim and crimp the edges as desired.
In a large mixing bowl, whisk together the granulated sugar, corn syrup, eggs, melted butter, vanilla extract, and salt until well combined.
Stir in the pecan halves until evenly coated in the filling mixture.
Pour the pecan filling into the prepared pie crust.

Bake the pie in the preheated oven for 40 to 50 minutes, or until the filling is set and the crust is golden brown.
If the crust begins to brown too quickly, you can cover the edges with foil halfway through baking.
Once baked, remove the pie from the oven and let it cool completely on a wire rack before slicing and serving.

Enjoy this delicious pecan pie on its own or with a dollop of whipped cream or a scoop of vanilla ice cream for a truly indulgent dessert!

Shortbread Cookies

Ingredients:

- 1 cup unsalted butter, softened
- 1/2 cup granulated sugar
- 2 cups all-purpose flour
- 1/4 teaspoon salt (optional)

Instructions:

    Preheat your oven to 350°F (175°C). Line a baking sheet with parchment paper.
    In a large mixing bowl, cream together the softened butter and granulated sugar until light and fluffy.
    Gradually add the flour to the butter mixture, mixing until well combined. The dough will be crumbly but should hold together when pressed.
    If desired, add the salt to the dough and mix until evenly distributed.
    Turn the dough out onto a lightly floured surface and knead it gently until it comes together into a smooth ball.
    Roll out the dough to about 1/4 inch thickness.
    Use cookie cutters to cut out shapes from the dough, or simply slice it into squares or rectangles.
    Place the cut-out cookies onto the prepared baking sheet, spacing them about 1 inch apart.
    Prick each cookie with a fork or toothpick to create a decorative pattern (optional).
    Bake the cookies in the preheated oven for 10 to 12 minutes, or until the edges are lightly golden.
    Remove the cookies from the oven and let them cool on the baking sheet for a few minutes before transferring them to a wire rack to cool completely.

Enjoy these classic shortbread cookies with a cup of tea or coffee, or decorate them with icing or chocolate for a special touch!

Buttermilk Pancakes

Ingredients:

- 1 1/2 cups all-purpose flour
- 2 tablespoons granulated sugar
- 1 teaspoon baking powder
- 1/2 teaspoon baking soda
- 1/4 teaspoon salt
- 1 1/4 cups buttermilk
- 1 large egg
- 2 tablespoons unsalted butter, melted
- 1 teaspoon vanilla extract
- Butter or oil for cooking

Instructions:

In a large mixing bowl, whisk together the flour, sugar, baking powder, baking soda, and salt.

In a separate bowl, whisk together the buttermilk, egg, melted butter, and vanilla extract until well combined.

Pour the wet ingredients into the dry ingredients and stir until just combined. It's okay if the batter is a little lumpy.

Preheat a non-stick skillet or griddle over medium heat and lightly grease with butter or oil.

Pour about 1/4 cup of batter onto the skillet for each pancake, spacing them apart to allow for spreading.

Cook the pancakes for 2-3 minutes, or until bubbles form on the surface and the edges look set.

Flip the pancakes with a spatula and cook for an additional 1-2 minutes, or until golden brown on the bottom.

Transfer the cooked pancakes to a plate and keep them warm while you cook the remaining batter.

Serve the pancakes warm with your favorite toppings, such as maple syrup, fresh berries, whipped cream, or chocolate chips.

Enjoy these fluffy and delicious buttermilk pancakes for a delightful breakfast or brunch!

Marble Cake

Ingredients:

For the vanilla batter:

- 1 and 1/2 cups all-purpose flour
- 1 and 1/2 teaspoons baking powder
- 1/4 teaspoon salt
- 1/2 cup unsalted butter, softened
- 3/4 cup granulated sugar
- 2 large eggs
- 1 teaspoon vanilla extract
- 1/2 cup milk

For the chocolate batter:

- 1/4 cup unsweetened cocoa powder
- 2 tablespoons hot water

Instructions:

Preheat your oven to 350°F (175°C). Grease and flour a 9x5-inch loaf pan or line it with parchment paper.

For the vanilla batter:

In a medium mixing bowl, whisk together the flour, baking powder, and salt. Set aside.
In a large mixing bowl, cream together the softened butter and granulated sugar until light and fluffy.
Beat in the eggs, one at a time, until well combined.
Stir in the vanilla extract.
Gradually add the dry ingredients to the wet ingredients, alternating with the milk, and mixing until just combined. Be careful not to overmix.

For the chocolate batter:

In a small bowl, mix together the cocoa powder and hot water until smooth to create a chocolate paste.

Assembling the marble cake:

Pour half of the vanilla batter into the prepared loaf pan, spreading it out evenly.
Spoon dollops of the chocolate paste onto the vanilla batter.
Use a knife or skewer to swirl the chocolate paste into the vanilla batter, creating a marble pattern.
Pour the remaining vanilla batter over the chocolate swirls and spread it out evenly.
Repeat the dolloping and swirling process with the remaining chocolate paste.
Use a knife or skewer to create more swirls on the top of the cake, if desired.
Bake in the preheated oven for 50-60 minutes, or until a toothpick inserted into the center of the cake comes out clean.
Allow the cake to cool in the pan for 10 minutes, then transfer it to a wire rack to cool completely before slicing and serving.

Enjoy this delicious and visually stunning marble cake as a delightful dessert or snack!

Apple Crisp

Ingredients:

For the apple filling:

- 6 cups apples, peeled, cored, and sliced (such as Granny Smith, Honeycrisp, or Fuji)
- 1/4 cup granulated sugar
- 2 tablespoons all-purpose flour
- 1 teaspoon ground cinnamon
- 1/4 teaspoon ground nutmeg
- 1 tablespoon lemon juice

For the crisp topping:

- 1 cup old-fashioned rolled oats
- 1/2 cup all-purpose flour
- 1/2 cup packed brown sugar
- 1/2 teaspoon ground cinnamon
- 1/4 teaspoon salt
- 1/2 cup unsalted butter, cold and cut into small pieces

Instructions:

Preheat your oven to 350°F (175°C). Grease a 9x13-inch baking dish or a similar-sized baking dish with butter or non-stick cooking spray.

For the apple filling:

In a large mixing bowl, combine the sliced apples, granulated sugar, flour, cinnamon, nutmeg, and lemon juice. Toss until the apples are evenly coated with the mixture.
Transfer the apple mixture to the prepared baking dish and spread it out evenly.

For the crisp topping:

In a separate mixing bowl, combine the rolled oats, flour, brown sugar, cinnamon, and salt.
Add the cold butter pieces to the oat mixture. Using your fingers or a pastry cutter, work the butter into the dry ingredients until the mixture resembles coarse crumbs and the butter is evenly distributed.

Sprinkle the crisp topping evenly over the apple mixture in the baking dish.
Bake in the preheated oven for 40-45 minutes, or until the topping is golden brown and the apples are tender and bubbly.
Remove the apple crisp from the oven and let it cool for a few minutes before serving.
Serve warm, optionally with a scoop of vanilla ice cream or a dollop of whipped cream.

Enjoy this delicious apple crisp as a comforting dessert on a chilly day!

Danish Pastries

Ingredients:

For the dough:

- 1 cup (240ml) whole milk, lukewarm
- 2 1/4 teaspoons (1 packet) active dry yeast
- 1/4 cup (50g) granulated sugar
- 1/2 teaspoon salt
- 2 large eggs
- 4 cups (500g) all-purpose flour
- 1 cup (225g) unsalted butter, cold

For the filling:

- Your choice of fruit preserves, custard, marzipan, or cream cheese

For the glaze (optional):

- 1 cup (120g) powdered sugar
- 2-3 tablespoons milk or water
- 1/2 teaspoon vanilla extract

Instructions:

In a small bowl, mix together the lukewarm milk, yeast, and a pinch of sugar. Let it sit for about 5-10 minutes until frothy.

In a large mixing bowl or the bowl of a stand mixer, combine the sugar, salt, eggs, and yeast mixture. Mix until well combined.

Gradually add the flour, mixing until a dough forms. If using a stand mixer, use a dough hook attachment and knead the dough for about 5-7 minutes until it becomes smooth and elastic. If kneading by hand, turn the dough out onto a lightly floured surface and knead for about 10 minutes.

Cut the cold butter into small cubes. Roll out the dough on a floured surface into a rectangle about 1/4 inch thick. Place the butter cubes evenly over two-thirds of the dough. Fold the unbuttered third over the middle third, then fold the remaining third over the top, like folding a letter.

Roll out the dough again into a rectangle, then fold it into thirds again. Repeat this process two more times, for a total of three times. This creates the layers that will give the pastry its flaky texture. Wrap the dough in plastic wrap and refrigerate for at least 1 hour, or overnight.

Preheat your oven to 400°F (200°C). Line baking sheets with parchment paper. Roll out the chilled dough on a floured surface into a large rectangle, about 1/4 inch thick. Cut the dough into squares or rectangles.

Place a spoonful of your desired filling in the center of each piece of dough. Fold the corners of the dough over the filling, pinching them together to seal.

Place the filled pastries on the prepared baking sheets, leaving some space between them. Let them rise for about 30 minutes.

Bake the pastries in the preheated oven for 15-20 minutes, or until they are golden brown and puffed up.

If desired, prepare the glaze by mixing together the powdered sugar, milk or water, and vanilla extract until smooth. Drizzle the glaze over the warm pastries. Allow the pastries to cool slightly before serving. Enjoy your homemade Danish pastries!

Feel free to customize the fillings and toppings according to your preference or include variations in your cookbook to inspire creativity among your readers!

Chocolate Eclairs

Ingredients:

For the choux pastry:

- 1/2 cup (120ml) water
- 1/2 cup (120ml) whole milk
- 1/2 cup (115g) unsalted butter, cut into small pieces
- 1 tablespoon granulated sugar
- 1/4 teaspoon salt
- 1 cup (125g) all-purpose flour
- 4 large eggs

For the pastry cream filling:

- 1 cup (240ml) whole milk
- 1/2 cup (100g) granulated sugar
- 4 large egg yolks
- 2 tablespoons cornstarch
- 1 teaspoon vanilla extract

For the chocolate icing:

- 4 ounces (115g) semisweet or bittersweet chocolate, chopped
- 1/2 cup (120ml) heavy cream
- 1 tablespoon unsalted butter

Instructions:

For the choux pastry:

Preheat your oven to 425°F (220°C). Line a baking sheet with parchment paper or a silicone baking mat.
In a medium saucepan, combine the water, milk, butter, sugar, and salt. Heat over medium heat until the mixture comes to a simmer and the butter is melted.

Reduce the heat to low and add the flour all at once. Stir vigorously with a wooden spoon until the mixture forms a smooth dough and pulls away from the sides of the pan.

Transfer the dough to a mixing bowl and let it cool for a few minutes. Then, add the eggs one at a time, beating well after each addition, until the dough is smooth and shiny.

Transfer the dough to a piping bag fitted with a large round tip. Pipe 4-inch long strips onto the prepared baking sheet, leaving space between them.

Bake the éclairs in the preheated oven for 15 minutes, then reduce the oven temperature to 375°F (190°C) and bake for an additional 10-15 minutes, or until golden brown and puffed. Remove from the oven and let them cool completely on a wire rack.

For the pastry cream filling:

In a saucepan, heat the milk until it just begins to simmer. In a separate bowl, whisk together the sugar, egg yolks, and cornstarch until smooth.

Gradually pour the hot milk into the egg mixture, whisking constantly. Return the mixture to the saucepan and cook over medium heat, whisking constantly, until thickened.

Remove from heat and stir in the vanilla extract. Transfer the pastry cream to a bowl and cover it with plastic wrap, pressing the wrap directly onto the surface of the cream to prevent a skin from forming. Refrigerate until chilled.

For the chocolate icing:

Place the chopped chocolate in a heatproof bowl. In a small saucepan, heat the cream until it just begins to simmer. Pour the hot cream over the chocolate and let it sit for a minute.

Add the butter to the chocolate mixture and stir until smooth and glossy. Let the icing cool slightly before using.

Assembly:

Once the éclairs and pastry cream are completely cooled, use a small knife to poke a hole in one end of each éclair.

Transfer the pastry cream to a piping bag fitted with a small round tip. Pipe the cream into the éclairs through the hole until they are filled.

Dip the top of each éclair into the chocolate icing or use a spoon to drizzle the icing over the top.

Place the filled and glazed éclairs on a serving platter and refrigerate until ready to serve.

Enjoy your homemade chocolate éclairs! They're best enjoyed fresh but can be stored in the refrigerator for a day or two.

Angel Food Cake

Ingredients:

- 1 cup (120g) cake flour
- 1 1/2 cups (300g) granulated sugar, divided
- 12 large egg whites, at room temperature
- 1 teaspoon cream of tartar
- 1/4 teaspoon salt
- 1 teaspoon vanilla extract
- 1/2 teaspoon almond extract (optional)
- Fresh berries, for serving (optional)
- Whipped cream, for serving (optional)

Instructions:

Preheat your oven to 350°F (175°C). Have ready an ungreased angel food cake pan (tube pan).
In a medium bowl, sift together the cake flour and half of the granulated sugar (3/4 cup). Set aside.
In a large mixing bowl or the bowl of a stand mixer fitted with the whisk attachment, beat the egg whites on medium speed until foamy.
Add the cream of tartar and salt to the egg whites and continue to beat on medium speed until soft peaks form.
Gradually add the remaining granulated sugar (3/4 cup), about 1-2 tablespoons at a time, while continuing to beat the egg whites on medium-high speed. Beat until stiff, glossy peaks form. Be careful not to overbeat.
Gently fold in the vanilla extract and almond extract (if using) with a rubber spatula.
Sprinkle the sifted flour mixture over the beaten egg whites in small batches, gently folding with the spatula after each addition until just combined. Be careful not to deflate the egg whites.
Spoon the batter into the ungreased angel food cake pan, smoothing the top with the spatula.
Bake in the preheated oven for 35-40 minutes, or until the top is golden brown and springs back when lightly touched.

Remove the cake from the oven and immediately invert the pan onto a cooling rack. Let the cake cool completely in the pan upside down. This helps prevent the cake from collapsing.
Once the cake is completely cooled, run a knife around the edges of the pan to loosen the cake. Gently remove the cake from the pan.
Serve the angel food cake slices with fresh berries and whipped cream if desired.

Enjoy your light and fluffy angel food cake! It's perfect for any occasion, from casual gatherings to elegant celebrations.

Fudgy Brownie Bars

Ingredients:

- 1 cup (230g) unsalted butter
- 2 cups (400g) granulated sugar
- 4 large eggs
- 1 teaspoon vanilla extract
- 3/4 cup (90g) unsweetened cocoa powder
- 1 cup (125g) all-purpose flour
- 1/2 teaspoon salt
- 1 cup (175g) semisweet chocolate chips

Instructions:

Preheat your oven to 350°F (175°C). Grease a 9x13-inch baking pan or line it with parchment paper, leaving some overhang for easy removal.

In a medium saucepan, melt the butter over medium heat. Remove from heat and stir in the granulated sugar until well combined.

Add the eggs one at a time, mixing well after each addition. Stir in the vanilla extract.

Sift the cocoa powder, flour, and salt into the saucepan with the butter mixture. Stir until just combined. Be careful not to overmix.

Fold in the chocolate chips until evenly distributed throughout the batter.

Pour the batter into the prepared baking pan and spread it out evenly with a spatula.

Bake in the preheated oven for 25-30 minutes, or until a toothpick inserted into the center comes out with a few moist crumbs. Be careful not to overbake, as you want the brownies to be fudgy.

Remove the pan from the oven and let the brownies cool completely in the pan on a wire rack.

Once cooled, use the parchment paper overhang to lift the brownies out of the pan. Cut into bars or squares.

Serve the fudgy brownie bars on their own or with a scoop of ice cream and a drizzle of chocolate sauce, if desired.

Store any leftover brownie bars in an airtight container at room temperature for up to 3 days, or in the refrigerator for longer storage.

Enjoy these indulgent fudgy brownie bars as a delightful treat for any occasion!

Raspberry Almond Tart

Ingredients:

For the crust:

- 1 1/4 cups (155g) all-purpose flour
- 1/4 cup (30g) almond flour
- 1/4 cup (50g) granulated sugar
- 1/2 cup (115g) unsalted butter, cold and cubed
- 1 large egg yolk
- 1-2 tablespoons ice water, as needed

For the almond filling:

- 1 cup (100g) almond flour
- 1/2 cup (100g) granulated sugar
- 1/4 teaspoon salt
- 1/2 cup (115g) unsalted butter, softened
- 2 large eggs
- 1 teaspoon almond extract

For the topping:

- 1/2 cup (75g) fresh raspberries
- 2 tablespoons sliced almonds
- Powdered sugar, for dusting

Instructions:

For the crust:

In a food processor, combine the all-purpose flour, almond flour, and granulated sugar. Pulse a few times to mix.
Add the cold, cubed butter and pulse until the mixture resembles coarse crumbs.
Add the egg yolk and 1 tablespoon of ice water. Pulse until the dough comes together, adding more ice water if needed.
Turn the dough out onto a lightly floured surface and knead it briefly until smooth. Shape the dough into a disk, wrap it in plastic wrap, and refrigerate for at least 30 minutes.

Preheat your oven to 375°F (190°C). Roll out the chilled dough on a lightly floured surface to fit a 9-inch tart pan. Press the dough into the bottom and up the sides of the pan. Trim any excess dough.

Prick the bottom of the crust with a fork. Line the crust with parchment paper and fill it with pie weights or dried beans.

Bake the crust in the preheated oven for 15 minutes. Remove the parchment paper and weights, then bake for an additional 5-7 minutes, or until lightly golden. Remove from the oven and let it cool slightly.

For the almond filling:

In a medium bowl, whisk together the almond flour, granulated sugar, and salt.

In a separate bowl, beat the softened butter until creamy. Add the eggs, one at a time, beating well after each addition. Stir in the almond extract.

Gradually add the almond flour mixture to the butter mixture, mixing until smooth and well combined.

Assembly:

Spread the almond filling evenly over the partially baked tart crust.

Arrange the fresh raspberries on top of the almond filling, pressing them gently into the filling.

Sprinkle the sliced almonds over the raspberries.

Bake the tart in the preheated oven for 25-30 minutes, or until the filling is set and the crust is golden brown.

Remove the tart from the oven and let it cool completely on a wire rack.

Before serving, dust the tart with powdered sugar.

Slice and serve the Raspberry Almond Tart, and enjoy the delicious combination of flavors and textures!

This tart is perfect for any occasion, from afternoon tea to elegant dinner parties. The almond filling provides a rich and nutty flavor that complements the sweetness of the raspberries beautifully.

Pistachio Biscotti

Ingredients:

- 1 3/4 cups (220g) all-purpose flour
- 1 teaspoon baking powder
- 1/4 teaspoon salt
- 1/2 cup (115g) unsalted butter, softened
- 3/4 cup (150g) granulated sugar
- 2 large eggs
- 1 teaspoon vanilla extract
- 1/2 cup (75g) shelled pistachios, roughly chopped
- 1/2 cup (75g) white chocolate chips or chunks (optional)

Instructions:

Preheat your oven to 350°F (175°C). Line a baking sheet with parchment paper.
In a medium bowl, sift together the all-purpose flour, baking powder, and salt. Set aside.
In a large mixing bowl or the bowl of a stand mixer, cream together the softened butter and granulated sugar until light and fluffy.
Add the eggs, one at a time, beating well after each addition. Stir in the vanilla extract.
Gradually add the dry ingredients to the wet ingredients, mixing until a dough forms. Fold in the chopped pistachios and white chocolate chips, if using, until evenly distributed.
Turn the dough out onto a lightly floured surface and divide it in half. Shape each half into a log about 12 inches long and 2 inches wide. Place the logs on the prepared baking sheet, spacing them apart.
Flatten the logs slightly with your hands to about 1/2 inch thickness.
Bake in the preheated oven for 25-30 minutes, or until the logs are lightly golden and firm to the touch.
Remove the baking sheet from the oven and let the logs cool for about 10 minutes.
Using a sharp knife, carefully slice the logs diagonally into 1/2 inch thick slices. Place the slices cut side down on the baking sheet.
Return the biscotti to the oven and bake for an additional 10-15 minutes, or until the biscotti are golden and crisp.

Remove from the oven and let the biscotti cool completely on a wire rack. Once cooled, the biscotti can be stored in an airtight container at room temperature for up to two weeks.

Enjoy your homemade Pistachio Biscotti with a cup of coffee or tea! They make a wonderful treat for any time of day, and their crunchy texture and nutty flavor are sure to delight your taste buds.

Blueberry Cobbler

Ingredients:

For the filling:

- 6 cups fresh blueberries
- 1/2 cup granulated sugar
- 1 tablespoon cornstarch
- 1 tablespoon freshly squeezed lemon juice
- 1 teaspoon lemon zest

For the topping:

- 1 1/2 cups all-purpose flour
- 1/2 cup granulated sugar
- 1 1/2 teaspoons baking powder
- 1/4 teaspoon salt
- 1/2 cup (1 stick) unsalted butter, cold and cut into small pieces
- 1/2 cup whole milk
- 1 teaspoon vanilla extract

For serving:

- Vanilla ice cream or whipped cream (optional)

Instructions:

Preheat your oven to 375°F (190°C). Grease a 9x13 inch baking dish or a similar-sized casserole dish.
In a large bowl, combine the fresh blueberries, granulated sugar, cornstarch, lemon juice, and lemon zest. Toss until the blueberries are evenly coated. Pour the mixture into the prepared baking dish and spread it out evenly.
In a separate bowl, whisk together the all-purpose flour, granulated sugar, baking powder, and salt.
Add the cold, cubed butter to the flour mixture. Using a pastry cutter or your fingers, cut the butter into the flour mixture until it resembles coarse crumbs.
In a small bowl, mix together the whole milk and vanilla extract. Pour the milk mixture into the flour mixture and stir until just combined. Be careful not to overmix.

Drop spoonfuls of the biscuit dough over the blueberry filling in the baking dish, covering the filling as evenly as possible.

Bake the cobbler in the preheated oven for 40-45 minutes, or until the topping is golden brown and the filling is bubbling.

Remove the cobbler from the oven and let it cool for a few minutes before serving.

Serve the blueberry cobbler warm, with vanilla ice cream or whipped cream if desired.

Enjoy the comforting flavors of this homemade blueberry cobbler, perfect for any occasion, especially when fresh blueberries are in season!

Black Forest Cake

Ingredients:

For the chocolate sponge cake:

- 1 3/4 cups (220g) all-purpose flour
- 3/4 cup (75g) unsweetened cocoa powder
- 2 cups (400g) granulated sugar
- 1 1/2 teaspoons baking powder
- 1 1/2 teaspoons baking soda
- 1 teaspoon salt
- 2 large eggs
- 1 cup (240ml) whole milk
- 1/2 cup (120ml) vegetable oil
- 2 teaspoons vanilla extract
- 1 cup (240ml) boiling water

For the cherry filling:

- 2 cups (500g) pitted cherries, fresh or canned
- 1/4 cup (50g) granulated sugar
- 1 tablespoon cornstarch
- 1 tablespoon water
- 1 tablespoon Kirsch (optional)

For the whipped cream:

- 2 cups (480ml) heavy cream, cold
- 1/4 cup (50g) powdered sugar
- 1 teaspoon vanilla extract

For garnish:

- Chocolate shavings or curls
- Maraschino cherries

Instructions:

1. Make the chocolate sponge cake:

    Preheat your oven to 350°F (175°C). Grease and flour two 9-inch round cake pans.
    In a large mixing bowl, sift together the all-purpose flour, cocoa powder, granulated sugar, baking powder, baking soda, and salt.
    Add the eggs, milk, vegetable oil, and vanilla extract to the dry ingredients. Beat on medium speed until well combined.
    Stir in the boiling water until the batter is smooth. The batter will be thin.
    Divide the batter evenly between the prepared cake pans.
    Bake in the preheated oven for 30-35 minutes, or until a toothpick inserted into the center of the cakes comes out clean.
    Remove the cakes from the oven and let them cool in the pans for 10 minutes. Then, transfer them to wire racks to cool completely.

2. Make the cherry filling:

    In a saucepan, combine the pitted cherries and granulated sugar. Cook over medium heat until the cherries release their juices and soften, about 5-7 minutes.
    In a small bowl, mix together the cornstarch and water to create a slurry. Stir the slurry into the cherry mixture.
    Cook, stirring constantly, until the cherry filling thickens, about 2-3 minutes.
    Remove the cherry filling from the heat and stir in the Kirsch, if using. Let it cool completely.

3. Make the whipped cream:

    In a large mixing bowl, beat the cold heavy cream, powdered sugar, and vanilla extract until stiff peaks form.

4. Assemble the Black Forest Cake:

    Once the cakes are completely cooled, use a long serrated knife to slice each cake horizontally into two layers.

Place one layer of cake on a serving platter. Spread a layer of whipped cream over the cake, followed by a layer of cherry filling.

Place another layer of cake on top and repeat the process until all the layers are used, finishing with a layer of whipped cream on top.

Use the remaining whipped cream to frost the sides of the cake.

Garnish the cake with chocolate shavings or curls and maraschino cherries.

Refrigerate the cake for at least 1-2 hours before serving to allow the flavors to meld together.

Slice and serve the Black Forest Cake, and enjoy the rich and indulgent flavors!

This classic dessert is sure to impress your guests with its beautiful layers and delicious combination of chocolate, cherries, and whipped cream.

Strawberry Swirl Cheesecake

Ingredients:

For the crust:

- 1 1/2 cups (150g) graham cracker crumbs
- 1/4 cup (50g) granulated sugar
- 1/2 cup (115g) unsalted butter, melted

For the cheesecake filling:

- 24 ounces (680g) cream cheese, softened
- 1 cup (200g) granulated sugar
- 3 large eggs
- 1 teaspoon vanilla extract
- 1/2 cup (120ml) sour cream
- 1/2 cup (120ml) heavy cream

For the strawberry swirl:

- 1 cup (150g) fresh strawberries, hulled and chopped
- 2 tablespoons granulated sugar
- 1 tablespoon lemon juice

Instructions:

For the crust:

> Preheat your oven to 325°F (160°C). Grease a 9-inch springform pan with butter or non-stick cooking spray.
> In a medium bowl, mix together the graham cracker crumbs, granulated sugar, and melted butter until well combined.
> Press the mixture evenly into the bottom of the prepared springform pan. Use the back of a spoon or a flat-bottomed glass to firmly press the crust into place.
> Bake the crust in the preheated oven for 10 minutes. Remove from the oven and let it cool while you prepare the cheesecake filling.

For the cheesecake filling:

In a large mixing bowl or the bowl of a stand mixer, beat the softened cream cheese until smooth and creamy.

Gradually add the granulated sugar and beat until well combined.

Add the eggs one at a time, beating well after each addition. Scrape down the sides of the bowl as needed.

Stir in the vanilla extract, sour cream, and heavy cream until smooth and creamy.

For the strawberry swirl:

In a blender or food processor, puree the chopped strawberries until smooth.

Transfer the strawberry puree to a small saucepan. Add the granulated sugar and lemon juice. Cook over medium heat, stirring constantly, until the mixture thickens slightly, about 5-7 minutes. Remove from heat and let it cool slightly.

Assembly:

Pour the cheesecake filling over the cooled crust in the springform pan, spreading it out evenly with a spatula.

Drop spoonfuls of the strawberry puree onto the cheesecake filling. Use a knife or toothpick to swirl the strawberry puree into the cheesecake filling, creating a marbled effect.

Place the springform pan on a baking sheet to catch any potential leaks, and bake the cheesecake in the preheated oven for 45-55 minutes, or until the edges are set and the center is slightly jiggly.

Turn off the oven and leave the cheesecake inside with the door slightly ajar for 1 hour to cool gradually.

Remove the cheesecake from the oven and let it cool completely at room temperature. Once cooled, refrigerate the cheesecake for at least 4 hours or overnight to set completely.

Before serving, run a knife around the edges of the cheesecake to loosen it from the pan. Remove the sides of the springform pan.

Slice the cheesecake into pieces and serve chilled. Enjoy the creamy texture and delicious strawberry swirl of this homemade cheesecake!

This Strawberry Swirl Cheesecake is perfect for any special occasion or as a delightful dessert to enjoy with family and friends.

Chocolate Soufflé

Ingredients:

- 4 ounces (115g) bittersweet or semisweet chocolate, chopped
- 3 tablespoons unsalted butter, plus more for greasing ramekins
- 1/4 cup (50g) granulated sugar, divided
- 3 large eggs, separated
- 1/4 teaspoon cream of tartar
- Pinch of salt
- 1/2 teaspoon vanilla extract
- Powdered sugar, for dusting (optional)

Instructions:

Preheat your oven to 375°F (190°C). Grease four 6-ounce ramekins with butter and coat them with granulated sugar, tapping out any excess sugar.

In a heatproof bowl set over a saucepan of simmering water, melt the chocolate and butter together, stirring until smooth. Remove from heat and let it cool slightly.

In a large mixing bowl, whisk together the egg yolks and half of the granulated sugar until pale and thick. Gradually whisk in the melted chocolate mixture and vanilla extract until well combined.

In a clean, dry mixing bowl, beat the egg whites with an electric mixer on medium speed until frothy. Add the cream of tartar and continue to beat until soft peaks form. Gradually add the remaining granulated sugar and a pinch of salt, beating on high speed until stiff peaks form.

Gently fold about one-third of the beaten egg whites into the chocolate mixture to lighten it. Then, carefully fold in the remaining egg whites until no white streaks remain, being careful not to deflate the mixture.

Divide the soufflé batter evenly among the prepared ramekins, filling them almost to the top.

Run your thumb around the inside edge of each ramekin to create a slight indentation, which will help the soufflés rise evenly.

Place the filled ramekins on a baking sheet and bake in the preheated oven for 12-15 minutes, or until the soufflés have risen and set, and the tops are lightly browned.

Dust the tops of the soufflés with powdered sugar, if desired, and serve immediately.

Enjoy the decadence of these chocolate soufflés, with their light, airy texture and intense chocolate flavor. Serve them warm for a delightful dessert experience!

Lemon Pound Cake

Ingredients:

- 1 1/2 cups all-purpose flour
- 1 teaspoon baking powder
- 1/4 teaspoon salt
- 1/2 cup unsalted butter, softened
- 1 cup granulated sugar
- 2 large eggs
- 1/2 cup milk
- Zest of 2 lemons
- Juice of 1 lemon
- 1 teaspoon vanilla extract

For the glaze:

- 1 cup powdered sugar
- Juice of 1 lemon
- Zest of 1 lemon

Instructions:

Preheat your oven to 350°F (175°C). Grease and flour a 9x5 inch loaf pan.
In a medium bowl, whisk together flour, baking powder, and salt. Set aside.
In a large mixing bowl, cream together the butter and sugar until light and fluffy, about 3-4 minutes.
Beat in the eggs one at a time, mixing well after each addition.
Stir in the lemon zest, lemon juice, and vanilla extract until well combined.
Gradually add the dry ingredients to the wet ingredients, alternating with the milk, beginning and ending with the dry ingredients. Mix until just combined, being careful not to overmix.
Pour the batter into the prepared loaf pan and spread it out evenly.
Bake in the preheated oven for 45-55 minutes, or until a toothpick inserted into the center comes out clean.
Allow the cake to cool in the pan for 10 minutes before transferring it to a wire rack to cool completely.

Once the cake has cooled, make the glaze by whisking together the powdered sugar, lemon juice, and lemon zest until smooth.
Drizzle the glaze over the cooled cake. Allow the glaze to set before slicing and serving.

Enjoy your delicious lemon pound cake!

Maple Pecan Bars

Ingredients:

For the crust:

- 1 1/2 cups all-purpose flour
- 1/2 cup unsalted butter, softened
- 1/4 cup granulated sugar
- 1/4 teaspoon salt

For the filling:

- 3/4 cup maple syrup
- 3/4 cup packed brown sugar
- 2 large eggs
- 1 tablespoon unsalted butter, melted
- 1 teaspoon vanilla extract
- 1/4 teaspoon salt
- 1 1/2 cups chopped pecans

Instructions:

Preheat your oven to 350°F (175°C). Grease and flour a 9x13 inch baking pan.
In a mixing bowl, combine the flour, softened butter, granulated sugar, and salt for the crust. Mix until crumbly.
Press the crust mixture evenly into the bottom of the prepared baking pan. Bake in the preheated oven for 15-20 minutes, or until lightly golden brown.
While the crust is baking, prepare the filling. In a separate bowl, whisk together the maple syrup, brown sugar, eggs, melted butter, vanilla extract, and salt until well combined.
Stir in the chopped pecans until evenly distributed.
Pour the filling mixture over the hot crust, spreading it out evenly.
Return the pan to the oven and bake for an additional 20-25 minutes, or until the filling is set.
Allow the bars to cool completely in the pan before slicing into squares.
Once cooled, slice into bars and serve. Enjoy the delicious maple pecan bars!

These bars are perfect for dessert or as a sweet treat with your morning or afternoon coffee.

Cherry Clafoutis

Ingredients:

- 1 tablespoon unsalted butter (for greasing the dish)
- 1 1/2 cups fresh cherries, pitted
- 3/4 cup whole milk
- 1/4 cup heavy cream
- 3 large eggs
- 1/2 cup granulated sugar
- 1 teaspoon vanilla extract
- 1/2 cup all-purpose flour
- Pinch of salt
- Powdered sugar, for dusting (optional)

Instructions:

Preheat your oven to 350°F (175°C). Grease a 9-inch round baking dish with the tablespoon of butter.
Arrange the pitted cherries evenly in the bottom of the baking dish.
In a blender or mixing bowl, combine the milk, heavy cream, eggs, granulated sugar, and vanilla extract. Blend or whisk until well combined.
Add the flour and salt to the mixture and blend or whisk until smooth. The batter will be thin.
Pour the batter over the cherries in the baking dish.
Bake in the preheated oven for 35-40 minutes, or until the clafoutis is puffed and golden brown on top, and a toothpick inserted into the center comes out clean.
Remove the clafoutis from the oven and let it cool for a few minutes.
Dust the top of the clafoutis with powdered sugar, if desired, before serving.
Serve the cherry clafoutis warm or at room temperature. Enjoy!

Cherry clafoutis is traditionally served as a dessert, but it's also delicious as a sweet breakfast treat or afternoon snack.

Almond Joy Cookies

Ingredients:

- 1 cup unsalted butter, softened
- 1 cup granulated sugar
- 1 cup packed brown sugar
- 2 large eggs
- 1 teaspoon vanilla extract
- 2 1/2 cups all-purpose flour
- 1 teaspoon baking soda
- 1/2 teaspoon baking powder
- 1/2 teaspoon salt
- 2 cups sweetened shredded coconut
- 1 cup semi-sweet chocolate chips
- 1 cup chopped almonds

Instructions:

Preheat your oven to 350°F (175°C). Line baking sheets with parchment paper or silicone baking mats.
In a large mixing bowl, cream together the softened butter, granulated sugar, and brown sugar until light and fluffy.
Beat in the eggs one at a time, then add the vanilla extract, mixing well after each addition.
In a separate bowl, whisk together the flour, baking soda, baking powder, and salt.
Gradually add the dry ingredients to the wet ingredients, mixing until just combined.
Stir in the shredded coconut, chocolate chips, and chopped almonds until evenly distributed throughout the dough.
Using a cookie scoop or tablespoon, drop rounded balls of dough onto the prepared baking sheets, spacing them about 2 inches apart.
Bake in the preheated oven for 10-12 minutes, or until the edges are golden brown and the cookies are set.
Allow the cookies to cool on the baking sheets for a few minutes before transferring them to a wire rack to cool completely.
Once cooled, store the Almond Joy cookies in an airtight container at room temperature.

Enjoy these delicious cookies with the classic flavors of Almond Joy candy bars!

Irish Soda Bread

Ingredients:

- 4 cups all-purpose flour
- 1 teaspoon baking soda
- 1 teaspoon salt
- 1 3/4 cups buttermilk
- Optional: 1 cup raisins or currants

Instructions:

Preheat your oven to 425°F (220°C). Lightly grease a baking sheet or line it with parchment paper.
In a large mixing bowl, whisk together the flour, baking soda, and salt.
If you're using raisins or currants, stir them into the dry ingredients.
Make a well in the center of the flour mixture and pour in most of the buttermilk. Mix the dough by hand or with a wooden spoon, adding more buttermilk as needed to form a soft, slightly sticky dough. Be careful not to overmix.
Turn the dough out onto a lightly floured surface and gently knead it a few times until it comes together into a round loaf. Don't knead too much, as soda bread doesn't require extensive kneading like yeast bread.
Shape the dough into a round loaf and place it on the prepared baking sheet. Use a sharp knife to score a deep cross in the top of the loaf.
Bake the bread in the preheated oven for 15 minutes, then reduce the heat to 400°F (200°C) and continue baking for another 25-30 minutes, or until the bread is golden brown and sounds hollow when tapped on the bottom.
Remove the bread from the oven and transfer it to a wire rack to cool completely before slicing and serving.
Serve the Irish soda bread with butter, jam, or any other toppings you prefer.

Enjoy your homemade Irish soda bread as a delicious accompaniment to soups, stews, or simply as a snack!

Cranberry Orange Scones

Ingredients:

- 2 cups all-purpose flour
- 1/3 cup granulated sugar
- 1 tablespoon baking powder
- 1/2 teaspoon salt
- Zest of 1 orange
- 1/2 cup (1 stick) unsalted butter, cold and cut into small pieces
- 1/2 cup dried cranberries
- 1/2 cup milk
- 1/4 cup freshly squeezed orange juice
- 1 teaspoon vanilla extract
- 1 large egg, lightly beaten

For the glaze (optional):

- 1 cup powdered sugar
- 2 tablespoons freshly squeezed orange juice
- Zest of 1 orange

Instructions:

Preheat your oven to 400°F (200°C). Line a baking sheet with parchment paper or a silicone baking mat.
In a large mixing bowl, whisk together the flour, granulated sugar, baking powder, salt, and orange zest.
Cut in the cold butter using a pastry cutter or your fingers until the mixture resembles coarse crumbs.
Stir in the dried cranberries.
In a separate bowl, whisk together the milk, orange juice, vanilla extract, and egg.
Gradually add the wet ingredients to the dry ingredients, stirring until just combined. Be careful not to overmix.
Turn the dough out onto a lightly floured surface and gently knead it a few times until it comes together.
Pat the dough into a circle about 1 inch thick. Use a sharp knife to cut the circle into 8 wedges.

Transfer the wedges to the prepared baking sheet, spacing them a few inches apart.

Bake in the preheated oven for 15-18 minutes, or until the scones are lightly golden brown.

While the scones are baking, prepare the glaze (if using) by whisking together the powdered sugar, orange juice, and orange zest until smooth.

Once the scones are done baking, remove them from the oven and let them cool on the baking sheet for a few minutes.

Drizzle the glaze over the warm scones, if desired.

Serve the cranberry orange scones warm or at room temperature. Enjoy!

These scones are best enjoyed fresh but can be stored in an airtight container at room temperature for up to 2 days.

Chocolate Babka

Ingredients:

For the dough:

- 4 cups all-purpose flour, plus more for dusting
- 1/2 cup granulated sugar
- 2 1/4 teaspoons (1 packet) active dry yeast
- 3/4 cup warm milk (about 110°F or 45°C)
- 2 large eggs, room temperature
- 1/2 cup unsalted butter, melted
- 1 teaspoon vanilla extract
- 1/2 teaspoon salt

For the chocolate filling:

- 1 cup semi-sweet chocolate chips or chopped chocolate
- 1/2 cup unsalted butter
- 1/2 cup powdered sugar
- 1/4 cup unsweetened cocoa powder
- 1 teaspoon ground cinnamon
- 1/2 teaspoon vanilla extract

For the syrup:

- 1/4 cup water
- 1/4 cup granulated sugar

Instructions:

In a small bowl, dissolve the yeast and 1 tablespoon of sugar in warm milk. Let it sit for about 5-10 minutes until frothy.
In a large mixing bowl or the bowl of a stand mixer fitted with a dough hook, combine the flour, remaining sugar, and salt.
Add the yeast mixture, melted butter, eggs, and vanilla extract to the flour mixture. Mix until a soft dough forms.

Knead the dough on a floured surface or in the stand mixer for about 5-7 minutes until it becomes smooth and elastic.

Place the dough in a greased bowl, cover with a clean kitchen towel, and let it rise in a warm place for about 1-2 hours or until doubled in size.

While the dough is rising, prepare the chocolate filling. In a saucepan, melt the butter and chocolate over low heat, stirring constantly until smooth. Remove from heat and stir in powdered sugar, cocoa powder, cinnamon, and vanilla extract until well combined. Set aside to cool slightly.

Once the dough has doubled in size, punch it down and divide it in half.

Roll out one half of the dough on a floured surface into a rectangle, about 1/4 inch thick.

Spread half of the chocolate filling evenly over the rolled-out dough, leaving a small border around the edges.

Roll up the dough tightly, starting from the long side, to form a log.

Repeat the process with the other half of the dough and remaining filling.

Carefully slice each log in half lengthwise to expose the filling, then twist the two pieces together, keeping the cut sides facing up.

Transfer the twisted dough into a greased loaf pan. Cover with a clean kitchen towel and let it rise again for about 30-45 minutes.

Preheat your oven to 350°F (175°C).

Bake the babka in the preheated oven for 30-35 minutes or until golden brown and cooked through.

While the babka is baking, prepare the syrup by combining water and sugar in a small saucepan. Bring to a boil, then remove from heat and let it cool slightly.

When the babka is done baking, brush the top with the syrup while it's still warm. Allow the babka to cool in the pan for about 10-15 minutes before transferring it to a wire rack to cool completely.

Once cooled, slice and serve. Enjoy your delicious chocolate babka!

You can store any leftover babka in an airtight container at room temperature for a few days or freeze it for longer storage.

Walnut Coffee Cake

Ingredients:

For the cake:

- 1/2 cup (1 stick) unsalted butter, softened
- 1 cup granulated sugar
- 2 large eggs
- 1 cup sour cream
- 1 teaspoon vanilla extract
- 2 cups all-purpose flour
- 1 teaspoon baking powder
- 1 teaspoon baking soda
- 1/2 teaspoon salt

For the walnut filling:

- 1 cup chopped walnuts
- 1/2 cup brown sugar
- 1 tablespoon ground cinnamon

For the streusel topping:

- 1/4 cup all-purpose flour
- 1/4 cup brown sugar
- 1/4 cup chopped walnuts
- 2 tablespoons unsalted butter, melted

Instructions:

Preheat your oven to 350°F (175°C). Grease and flour a 9x13 inch baking pan.
In a mixing bowl, cream together the softened butter and granulated sugar until light and fluffy.
Beat in the eggs, one at a time, until well combined. Stir in the sour cream and vanilla extract.
In a separate bowl, whisk together the flour, baking powder, baking soda, and salt. Gradually add the dry ingredients to the wet ingredients, mixing until just combined.

In another bowl, prepare the walnut filling by mixing together the chopped walnuts, brown sugar, and ground cinnamon.

Spread half of the cake batter into the prepared baking pan. Sprinkle the walnut filling evenly over the batter.

Spoon the remaining batter over the walnut filling and spread it out evenly.

In a small bowl, prepare the streusel topping by combining the flour, brown sugar, chopped walnuts, and melted butter. Mix until crumbly.

Sprinkle the streusel topping over the top of the cake batter.

Bake in the preheated oven for 35-40 minutes, or until a toothpick inserted into the center comes out clean.

Allow the walnut coffee cake to cool in the pan for 10 minutes before transferring it to a wire rack to cool completely.

Once cooled, slice the coffee cake into squares and serve.

Enjoy this delicious walnut coffee cake with your favorite hot beverage for a delightful treat!

Orange Creamsicle Cupcakes

Ingredients:

For the cupcakes:

- 1 1/2 cups all-purpose flour
- 1 1/2 teaspoons baking powder
- 1/4 teaspoon salt
- 1/2 cup (1 stick) unsalted butter, softened
- 1 cup granulated sugar
- 2 large eggs
- 1 teaspoon vanilla extract
- 1/2 cup freshly squeezed orange juice
- Zest of 1 orange
- 1/4 cup milk

For the frosting:

- 1/2 cup (1 stick) unsalted butter, softened
- 2 cups powdered sugar
- 1 teaspoon vanilla extract
- 2-3 tablespoons freshly squeezed orange juice
- Orange food coloring (optional)
- Orange zest for garnish (optional)

Instructions:

Preheat your oven to 350°F (175°C). Line a muffin tin with cupcake liners.
In a medium bowl, whisk together the flour, baking powder, and salt. Set aside.
In a large mixing bowl, cream together the softened butter and granulated sugar until light and fluffy.
Beat in the eggs, one at a time, until well combined. Stir in the vanilla extract.
Add the flour mixture to the wet ingredients in three additions, alternating with the orange juice and zest, beginning and ending with the flour mixture. Mix until just combined.
Stir in the milk until the batter is smooth.

Divide the batter evenly among the prepared cupcake liners, filling each about 2/3 full.

Bake in the preheated oven for 18-20 minutes, or until a toothpick inserted into the center of a cupcake comes out clean.

Allow the cupcakes to cool in the muffin tin for a few minutes before transferring them to a wire rack to cool completely.

While the cupcakes are cooling, prepare the frosting. In a mixing bowl, beat together the softened butter, powdered sugar, vanilla extract, and orange juice until smooth and creamy. Add more orange juice if needed to reach your desired consistency. Optionally, add orange food coloring for a more vibrant color.

Once the cupcakes are completely cooled, frost them with the orange frosting using a piping bag or offset spatula.

Garnish the frosted cupcakes with orange zest, if desired.

Serve and enjoy these delicious orange creamsicle cupcakes!

These cupcakes are perfect for parties, gatherings, or just as a sweet treat for any occasion.